DISCARDED

six words, many turtles,
and three days in hong kong

six words,
many turtles,
and three days
in hong kong

by Patricia McMahon

with photographs by Susan G. Drinker

Houghton Mifflin Company
Boston 1997

Text copyright © 1997 by Patricia McMahon

Photographs copyright © 1997 by Susan G. Drinker

Maps copyright © 1997 by Geoffrey Ganter

Special thanks to the Asia Society of Houston for providing proper Chinese pronunciations.

For information about this and other Houghton Mifflin trade and reference books and multimedia products, visit The Bookstore at Houghton Mifflin on the World Wide Web at http://www.hmco.com/trade/.

The text of this book is set in 13 pt. Joanna.

Library of Congress Cataloging-in-Publication Data

McMahon, Patricia.

Six words, many turtles, and three days in Hong Kong / by Patricia McMahon; with photographs by Susan G. Drinker.

p. cm.

Summary: Describes the daily activities, school work, and family life of an eight-year-old Chinese girl living in Hong Kong.

ISBN 0-395-68621-0

1. Family—Hong Kong. 2. Hong Kong—Social life and customs. [1. Family life—Hong Kong. 2. Hong Kong—Description and travel.] I. Drinker, Susan, ill. II. Title.

HQ687.M43 1997

306.85'095125—dc21 96-44191 CIP AC

Printed in Singapore

TWP 10 9 8 7 6 5 4 3 2 1

This book is for my sister, Mary McMahon—

good friend, fellow traveler, runner from rhinos.

—P.M.

To Paul Caponigro—

for whom presence is more than a way of being, and

in whose presence I became more than a photographer.

—S.G.D.

acknowledgments

I WISH TO ACKNOWLEDGE, WITH GRATITUDE, THE OPEN, enthusiastic, and warm friendliness of the Law family—Yi Fau, Lai Man, and of course, Tsz Yan. I remain astonished by their goodhearted and good-humored willingness to go above and beyond, for both Susan Drinker and myself. They are new friends in a well-loved place.

This book would not have been possible without the great generosity of Mrs. Cecelia Wong. I am humbly in her debt and send her my sincere thanks. A thank-you as well to her daughter, Pat Proctor, my friend from Seoul.

The Hong Kong adventure was greatly aided and abetted by the hospitality and forbearance of the Long family: Margy, George, Katherine, and the pirate, Graham. I must thank them for a place of shelter, great food, rude awakenings, and so much more. *Kamsahamnida.*

Our excursion was made possible by the assistance of Betty and Dan McCarthy, who came and stayed. I thank them with love. The same goes to Joseph McCarthy, fellow lover of Hong Kong, and to Conor Clarke McCarthy, who at two years of age tried to buy the Star Ferry, and who can send Mother's Day all the way around the world.

I am grateful to my editor, Karen Klockner, who keeps fighting the good fight with me; to Kim Keller at Houghton Mifflin for her kind words and support; to Amy Drinker, who sent us Susan; to Peggy Martin for her last-minute ride to the rescue; and to Allyn Dukes and Leona Bernard.

how to pronounce
some of the words in this book:

Names of people:

Tsz Yan (tss yenn)

Lai Man (ly mann)

Yi Fau (ee faw)

Chak Fung (chock fung)

Ka Kit (kaw kit)

Ho Ying (hoe ying)

Kwan Poi (kwann poy)

Names of places:

Tuen Mun (twen munn)

Siu Hong (see-ew hong)

Kwai Chung (kwy chung)

Kowloon (cow loon)

Names of things:

sampan (saam paan)

dim sum (dim summ)

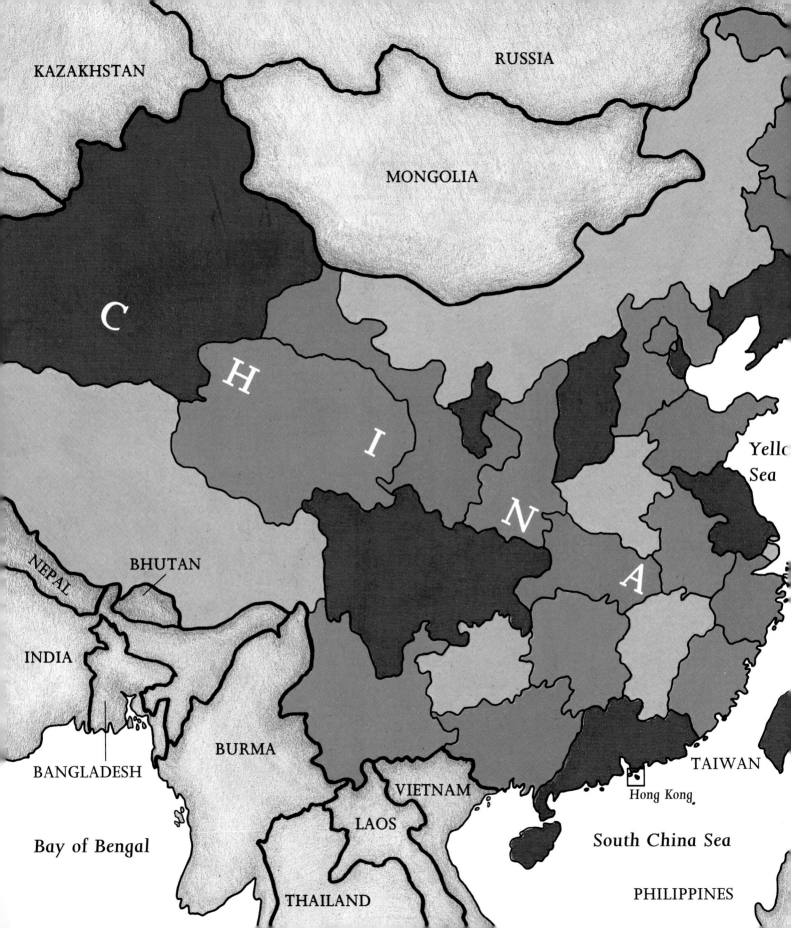

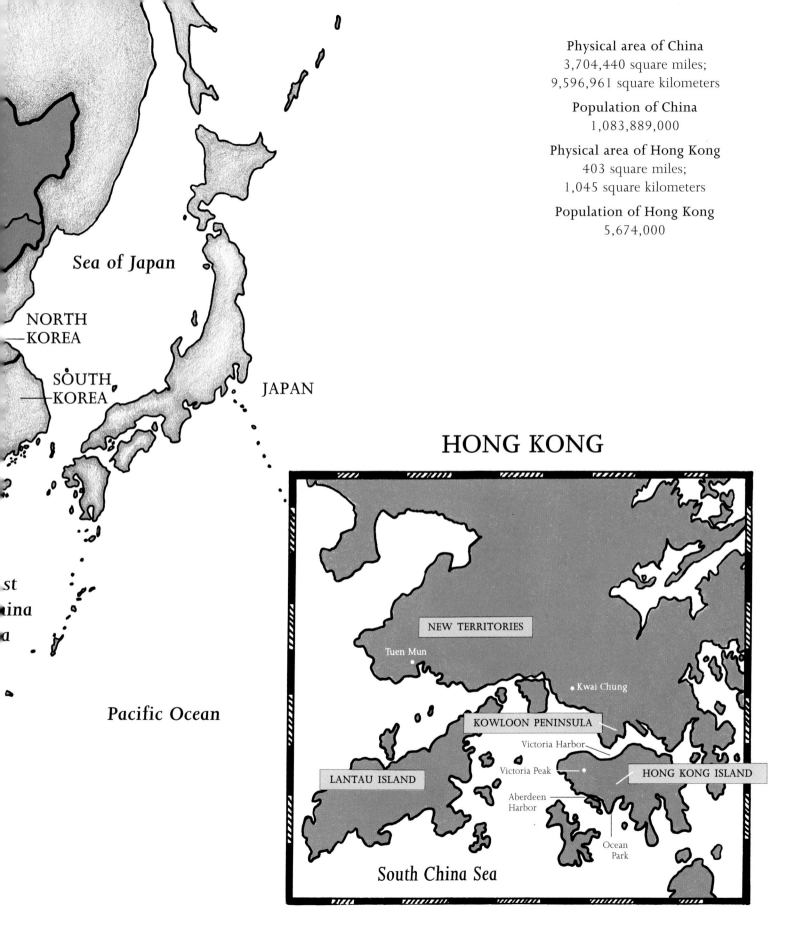

Physical area of China
3,704,440 square miles;
9,596,961 square kilometers

Population of China
1,083,889,000

Physical area of Hong Kong
403 square miles;
1,045 square kilometers

Population of Hong Kong
5,674,000

Sea of Japan

NORTH
KOREA

SOUTH
KOREA

JAPAN

Pacific Ocean

st

ina

a

HONG KONG

NEW TERRITORIES

Tuen Mun

Kwai Chung

KOWLOON PENINSULA

Victoria Harbor

LANTAU ISLAND

Victoria Peak

HONG KONG ISLAND

Aberdeen
Harbor

Ocean
Park

South China Sea

ROUND AND ROUND and round again. Tsz Yan watches two girls running, one trying to catch the other in today's game. Nearby, two boys from her class do the same, running fast. One tries to catch the other before he can get to the gap in the circle. Everyone wonders if the chaser will catch the chased. Not everyone hopes to be the next one chosen, but some do.

Eight-year-old Tsz Yan, whose English name is Vivian, laughs as she sees a runner shoot past the spot where he could be safe. She won't make that mistake, she decides. She'll run so fast she'll be the fastest ever. Tsz Yan is so busy thinking about what to do if she's chosen that she forgets to pay attention to the girl who is slowly pacing the circle. Suddenly the girl chooses Tsz Yan. Caught by surprise, Tsz Yan scrambles up, knowing she'll never catch the runner. But then the end-of-school bell rings. Saved.

Tsz Yan heads to the school bags, all lined up, waiting for their owners. The green one with the orange cat whose English name is Garfield belongs to her. With care, Tsz Yan lifts the too-heavy bag onto her back. She is sure that one of these days she is going to put it on and fall flat on her back. Tsz Yan thinks she will look like a turtle on its back, legs moving, going nowhere. Today, at least, she remains on her feet, joining the other students as they head in orderly fashion for the exit.

They come out into the noisy bustle of school changing time at the Taoist Ching Chung Academy in Tuen Mun, Hong Kong. These students have been at school since 6:30 in the morning and are leaving at 12:30. Another five hundred students are coming to begin their school day. Students pour out of school and students pour in. Buses drop students off, pick others up, honk and beep as they try to turn around in the small, narrow streets. Grown-ups call out to small children to be careful.

Schoolchildren are everywhere. Younger brothers and sisters are everywhere. So are mothers and grandmothers. A few older people watch just for fun. The girls and boys of the security patrol, wearing their red berets, try to keep order.

Tsz Yan boards the bus with other children from her neighborhood, all going home to the Siu Hong Apartments. The tall red-brown buildings, twenty of them standing all together, can be seen easily from almost anywhere in Tuen Mun. The buildings seem to reach up to the sky, but the mountains of Hong Kong reach even higher. Like Tsz Yan, some of the students on the bus wear the green shorts and white shirt uniform for gym days. Others wear the dress uniform of a plaid skirt or shorts with a white shirt. All the students carry the too-heavy backpacks with pictures of Snoopy or Mickey Mouse or Donald Duck or maybe Hello Kitty. Each student also carries a water bottle. At the Taoist Ching Chung Academy, everyone has to bring his or her own water for the school day. Tsz Yan carries her bottle in a bright red bag with a picture of Minnie Mouse on it. She likes Minnie Mouse. There is a big statue of Minnie Mouse from Disneyland in Tokyo that stands on the bookcase in her home, keeping guard while everyone is away all day.

From the windows of the bus, Tsz Yan sees the tall buildings, busy roads, canals, and trains that are all part of her city, Tuen Mun. Tuen Mun is in a section of Hong Kong called the New Territories.

They are called "new" because the British leased them from China in 1898 for a period of ninety-nine years. The other parts of Hong Kong, which include Hong Kong Island, the Kowloon Peninsula, and other islands, became British territories between 1841 and 1860, so they are the "old" territories. Tsz Yan has always found it funny that the New Territories have been called "new" for almost one hundred years.

The New Territories run all the way up from Kowloon to Hong Kong's border with China. Hong Kong is a neighbor of China, a small one sitting on the edge of the South China Sea, next to one of the biggest countries in the world. But now Hong Kong is going to become part of China.

When Hong Kong becomes part of China, Tsz Yan, her family, her classmates, her neighbors, and her friends will not suddenly become Chinese. They already are Chinese. They are Chinese residents of Hong Kong. But Hong Kong will no longer be a part of Great Britain. Hong Kong will become part of China, and no one knows exactly what this will mean for the people who live in Hong Kong.

The grown-ups around Tsz Yan have been discussing this for a long time. Tsz Yan and her friends think about it, too, but not as much as the grown-ups do. China is an enormous place, so big, so much its own. Hong Kong is a smaller place. So everyone wonders, will Hong Kong still be itself when it becomes part of something so big? And is a Chinese person living in Hong Kong the same as a Chinese person living in China?

Tsz Yan's mother and father are not very worried. To them,

China is not a strange, faraway land. China is where Tsz Yan's father works every day. Law, Yi Fau, whose English name is Paul, leaves Tuen Mun every Monday for the factory in China where he works. He comes home again on Saturday—home to his daughter, Tsz Yan, and his wife, Lai Man, whose English name is Anita.

Tsz Yan turns her thoughts away from the riddle of China. She hears two friends from the singing group at school practicing a new song. She joins in. "Sing, sing, sing—Sing, merrily, sing." Tsz Yan loves singing with the group, which has won prizes singing in both English and Chinese. The music teacher says "merrily" is an English word that means "having a good time." Tsz Yan knows she will be feeling merrily tomorrow, for there is no school. And her father is coming home.

The bus arrives at the Siu Hong Apartments. A few mothers or grandmothers meet the bus and are quickly handed heavy school bags. Most of the children scatter on their own. Some head home to lunch and homework. Some have lunch near the supermarket in a restaurant that has tables set up in the hallway. Tsz Yan and a friend trudge on with their packs. They meet the friend's mother, whose arms are filled with a new baby. Tsz Yan's mother is still at work.

After school every day, Tsz Yan walks to the apartment of Mrs. Tong, who takes care of Tsz Yan until her mother comes home. Mrs. Tong's apartment is in a building that looks exactly like Tsz Yan's building. And Mrs. Tong's apartment looks exactly like Tsz Yan's, except it has Mrs. Tong's furniture and

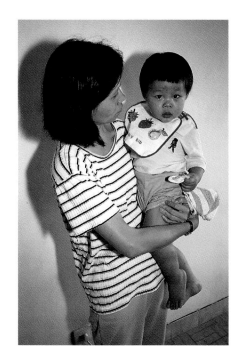

belongings in it. When Tsz Yan leaves for school each morning, her mother leaves for work in Kwai Chung, another city in the New Territories. Lai Man works in the office of a company that has a factory in China. The factory makes clothing for people in Europe.

Mrs. Tong makes lunch while Tsz Yan plays with Chak Fung; he and his sister also stay with Mrs. Tong while their parents are at work. Chak Fung's sister goes to afternoon school, so Tsz Yan almost never sees her. Chak Fung brings his shoes to Tsz Yan. He knows that shoes mean he's going out, and he hopes Tsz Yan will put them on for him, since Mrs. Tong would not. But it's not time for going outside. It's time for Tsz Yan to have lunch and do homework and for Chak Fung to take a nap.

Tsz Yan takes the great pile of books from her backpack. She puts her English homework on the bottom and begins to work her way

down. First Health. Today there are horrible pictures of diseases people can catch if they're not careful. She has to match the picture of the disease with the thing that can cause it. She circles a picture of a large rat. What trouble is he causing? This must be important to learn, Tsz Yan thinks, but it is not much fun to look at.

Math homework comes next, but it has to wait. Tsz Yan doesn't understand what she has to do. Neither does Mrs. Tong. Tsz Yan does her geography assignment and then moves on to her Chinese homework. Tsz Yan begins to practice her characters, writing each one carefully. There are

so many Chinese characters that Tsz Yan wonders if she will ever learn them all. Her family's friend, Mrs. Wong, who says she is old and who Tsz Yan knows is very smart, still doesn't know them all. There are tens of thousands of Chinese characters in all. Tsz Yan thinks that someone who knows them all must be both very old and very smart.

Taking a break, Tsz Yan looks out the Tong's window, far down to the courtyard below. Some children are already outside playing. Tsz Yan wants to go out, but she has to wait for her mother. Most afternoons Tsz Yan does her homework, walks home with her mother for dinner, and then does some more homework before bed. But today Tsz Yan knows she'll be able to play; there will be plenty of time to finish her homework over the weekend.

She picks up her English homework. English has twenty-six

characters, called letters, and the letters make an alphabet. Twenty-six characters should be easier to learn than thousands, but Chinese is Tsz Yan's language, and the characters make sense because they represent the words she speaks. Tsz Yan often sees and hears English words because of Hong Kong's connection to England. She wonders if English words will slowly slip away when Hong Kong becomes part of China. Then, she thinks, maybe she will not have so much English homework to do.

Tsz Yan's father tells her all the time that English helps him with his job. And her mother says English helps her in her work in the office in Kwai Chung. "No matter what," they tell her, "study English." Tsz Yan has been studying English since she was five years old. Not always merrily, but always studying.

Today Tsz Yan is studying six words she has to learn by Monday.

In her workbook she reads a story about a boy who is afraid of a big dog. He is worried his friends will think he is silly for being scared. But he is wrong. They go off in a noisy group to one of their homes, where the hungry friends eat chicken wings and jellyfish.

Tsz Yan likes this story because any list of her favorite foods would include chicken wings and jellyfish. Jellyfish might even be at the top of her list. But then again, anything at McDonald's might be, too. There is a McDonald's in Tuen Mun Centre that Tsz Yan always wants to go to. Her parents never want to go there. Tsz Yan writes the words she must learn this weekend. HAPPY, HUNGRY, FRIEND, SCARED, FAMILY, NOISY. As she writes, she thinks the boy might have been happier if his friends had taken him to McDonald's.

Tsz Yan begins to write the word HAPPY over and over in a column. Write it and understand it—that's what she's supposed to do. She will be HAPPY when her homework is finished, she knows. She would be very HAPPY if she never had to do homework. She is most HAPPY when she and her mother and father are all together. As she fills in the list, she thinks about last weekend. Her family went to the library. Tsz Yan's parents found some books for her with words in both English and Chinese. And Tsz Yan found a book about a Chinese princess with robes as blue as the sky behind the mountains above the Siu Hong Apartments.

Chak Fung wakes from his nap, beginning

again his over-and-over game of soccer. Kick and chase, kick and chase. Tsz Yan begins the over-and-over game of writing HUNGRY. But then her mother, Lai Man, arrives before she can finish. HAPPY to see her mother, Tsz Yan puts HUNGRY away to finish later.

Tsz Yan asks her mother over and again if she may please play outside when they get home. She asks as they pass ladies airing their quilts in the afternoon sun. She asks as they pass a con-

fused boy who isn't sure he likes his bicycle. Her mother says she'll think about it because there is still more homework to be done. Again Tsz Yan asks as they pass the every-afternoon soccer game and the gang of young fish trappers who make great plans but never catch any fish. She asks once more while they wait for an elevator. Lai Man finally agrees as the elevator door opens on their floor. Standing in front of them is their neighbor, Ka Kit, whose English

name is Jackie, balancing his bicycle, waiting for an elevator to take him downstairs to play.

Quick as she can, Tsz Yan changes her clothes, finds her badminton racket, and wheels her bicycle through the dark halls. In a flash she is racing Ka Kit around the courtyard. The badminton game has to wait while he races as fast as the elevator will take him to find his black racket. He won't play with Tsz Yan's pink ones. Pretending there is a net, they play against each other and some friends, giving each other high-fives when they score.

After badminton, the two friends wander from courtyard to courtyard through the busy afternoon at Siu Hong Apartments.

Afternoon students come home. Small children ride or walk with mothers and grandmothers. Old men carry birdcages, taking their pets for a walk, stopping to visit with friends while the birds sing to each other. Tsz Yan and Ka Kit end up at the large pond, the one with orange fish and many turtles. They wait for the turtle man. He always comes. Every afternoon the old man brings bread to the turtle pond. The turtles seem to know he's coming. They swim up, a great group of them, and take bread from his hand.

Today the turtle man teaches Tsz Yan and Ka Kit how to hold the bread out patiently. While Ka Kit holds it steady, a turtle takes bread from his hand. Tsz Yan wonders if the turtles think bread and fingers are tasty together. A little boy watches worriedly. *Snap!* Tsz Yan's bread disappears into a turtle's mouth. The little boy claps his hands.

Later that evening, after dinner, after dark, Tsz Yan finishes her HUNGRY list. She promises Lai Man she will do two more

words tomorrow and also on Sunday. Tsz Yan sits at her table, which is usually folded to make space in the small, but big enough, apartment. HUNGRY. Tsz Yan knows she is not HAPPY when she is HUNGRY. HUNGRY is what turtles are when they see bread. Or do they smell bread? They surely eat bread, Tsz Yan knows, remembering the turtle's mouth coming so close to her fingers. Finishing the list, tired but not HUNGRY, Tsz Yan heads for bed. Sleepy thoughts fill her head. Do little turtles like to eat at McDonald's? Do they carry backpacks on their shells? She falls asleep. Minnie Mouse watches over all.

• • •

When Tsz Yan wakes to a new day, she hears a different sound. There are two people talking. Her father is home from China. HAPPY and HUNGRY, sharing food with two, not one, Tsz Yan realizes that soon she will not have to say her father is

home from China. The Siu Hong Apartments will be in China. But right now, her father is not in China. He is home for the weekend, and he has a very good idea.

He suggests a family outing to Hong Kong Island, where there is a famous and wonderful amusement park. Tsz Yan has only been to Ocean Park once before. She has been waiting for the day she could go again. Tsz Yan's best friend and cousin, Ho Ying, whose English name is Joanne, will come along to share the fun.

The excursion begins with a walk to the LRT, which is a small train connecting parts of Tuen Mun with each other and connecting Tuen Mun with different cities in the New Territories. This helps the many families like the Laws who do not own a car. But, as Tsz Yan's father says, pointing at the long train, they have many cars! After riding on the LRT, the family heads for the ferry to Hong Kong Island. The sea between Tuen Mun and Victoria

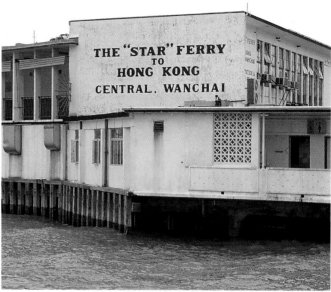

Harbor is filled with every kind of boat. Tsz Yan and Ho Ying watch great boats loaded with cargo setting out for trips across the ocean. Fishing boats and shrimpers are on the water. Small Chinese junks share the harbor with ferries and large new junks designed for pleasure boating.

While her mother and father catch up on a week's worth of talk, Tsz Yan teaches Ho Ying a new song in English. It's about a flower called edelweiss. Tsz Yan thinks the song moves slowly but has a pretty tune. Ho Ying likes the "Sing, sing, sing" song better. Tsz Yan remembers that edelweiss is a flower from Europe, and she imagines people skiing down mountains there, in her mother's factory's clothing, singing "Edelweiss."

As the family comes into Victoria Harbor, they

see tall buildings everywhere. The Star Ferry goes back and forth between Kowloon and the harbor. The group walks from the pier to the bus station. They pass people, people, and more people. Men and women in business suits, talking on phones, rush by. Women sit selling vegetables. A man cuts hair outside next to a woman selling flowers. At the end of an alley, a small altar is set up,

with incense sticks burning softly. All around, Tsz Yan sees new buildings being built and old ones being torn down. There is so little space for building on Hong Kong Island that something old has to come down before something new can go up. Victoria Peak, the famous mountain of Hong Kong, rises above all the noise and bustle.

As the bus carries them along, the two cousins bounce on their seats. They laugh as they arrive at Ocean Park with the many other Saturday visitors. There is so much to do, Tsz Yan and Ho Ying

can hardly choose. They look at the map, pointing here and there. They begin to run, not knowing where they are going. Lai Man directs them toward the park tram. They board with a mixed group of Chinese people, Korean people, Indian people, Filipino people, English people, a tall lady who looks American, and people who look English but don't sound it. Tsz Yan hums "Edelweiss" to see if anyone knows it.

The girls go on every ride once, some twice. They each try the canoes by themselves, and then ride together in one canoe. They ride the pink train together while Tsz Yan's parents take a separate car. They shoot at each other with their hands, pretending to be cowboys. The girls and Lai Man cannot stop laughing as Yi Fau dies several loud deaths. They keep laughing when he climbs aboard an airplane shaped like a pig, made for someone much smaller than he is.

From one ride to another they go. A cable car, high up the mountainside, takes them to another part of the park. The car shakes and shimmies. Tsz Yan worries that they will fall far down, landing in the South China Sea. She doesn't want to look down but she makes herself do it. Ho Ying points out Aberdeen Harbor, where families live on *sampan* boats. Lai Man points out the floating restaurants, waiting for night to make their many-colored lights shine. Yi Fau sees an empty car going

in the other direction; he shades his eyes as he searches far below for the missing passengers. He can make Tsz Yan and her mother laugh all the time.

Lai Man wants the girls to stop for lunch even though they can hardly sit still. The food stand offers dishes from all over Asia. Tsz Yan's mother and father pick *nasi goreng*, a rice dish from Indonesia. The girls worry about what to get, considering Chinese buns with barbecued pork, but deciding in the end to have Japanese food—with American Cokes.

Then it's quick—on to the famous water show. The announcer talks to the crowd in both English and Chinese. Tsz Yan understands some of one and all of the other. The sea lions are silly, their trainer sillier. Dolphins race around the pool, leaping up and down as they go. And then a whale, all black and white, leaps out of the water over a brave man below. Tsz Yan is amazed as the man rides on the whale's nose, heading up to the sky. They seem to reach as high as Victoria Peak.

The day goes from good to better to best. In a part of the park made to look like China did long ago, the family stops to watch a show in the village square. The cousins admire the dancers and hold their breath as a man stands barefoot on knives. Standing in a replica of old China, Tsz Yan remembers again that she will soon be living in a new part of China. Her father takes her picture at the foot of a giant statue of Buddha near the square. Tsz Yan feels so small standing there, as small as Hong Kong must look against the bigness of China. But as small as she is, Tsz Yan doesn't feel any less herself. Maybe small Hong Kong can be itself, even with China towering over it.

Then it's time to head home by bus and boat and train, all the way to the Siu Hong Apartments. Ho Ying leaves, which makes Tsz Yan sad. And the homework is still waiting. She starts to write a line of words, top to bottom: FRIEND, FRIEND, FRIEND. Tsz Yan knows that Ho Ying is her FRIEND. Today would not have been as much fun if Ho Ying had not been along. The two have been playing together since they were small, yet they like each other still. And Ka Kit is my FRIEND, Tsz Yan thinks, writing down the page. And the turtle man is the turtles' FRIEND. And FRIEND is such a big word that even a whale and a man can be friends.

Almost too tired, she begins to work on the chain of SCARED. SCARED can be a big word and a small word, Tsz Yan decides. When the cable car left the station today—dropping slightly and then climbing high—she was very SCARED, a big SCARED. She remembers that she was SCARED when she fed the turtles the other day, but less so than on the cable car ride. When the man stood on knives she was SCARED that he would cut his feet. She was also a little SCARED when they went into the store filled with candies— SCARED that her parents might be just looking and not buying. But that was only a small scare, not lasting long, because they all walked away

with sweets in hands and mouths. Now Tsz Yan is a little SCARED she will fall asleep before she finishes her list. But finish it she does, falling asleep, head in hands, only after the last word is written.

• • •

In Tsz Yan's family, Sunday morning means it's time for dim sum. Dim sum is a word that describes stuffed buns and dumplings; it has also come to mean the meal at which these foods are served. So Sunday morning finds Tsz Yan hopping and skipping a game across the pavement, just ahead of her parents, as they head to the Fountainview Restaurant. In the center of the Siu Hong Apartments is a building that houses a small grocery store, a small restaurant with tables in the hall, small stores selling almost everything, a market area, and the Fountainview Restaurant.

So many of the many people who live in Siu Hong go for dim sum that the Laws have to wait for a table. After a while they're shown to a table in a large room filled with other families. In the aisles between the tables are the dim sum ladies. These women push carts around, each cart carrying a different type of dim sum and other good foods to eat. Everyone can pick and choose what they want from the carts, which are piled high with flower rolls, buns with date filling, buns with barbecued pork filling (like the ones at Ocean Park), pork dumplings, crabmeat dumplings, and shrimp dumplings. There are ladies who have bowls piled high with shiny squid, covered bowls filled with rice, and much more. Everyone talks, calls to friends, orders loudly.

Tsz Yan's favorite food of all goes rolling by. She wants to order some. Her mother tries to talk her out of it. Tsz Yan talks her mother into it. Adding her voice to the many others, Tsz Yan orders a small bowl of French fries with a hot dog perched on top. Her parents tell her every week that French fries are not proper dim sum. But Tsz Yan thinks it's very good dim sum, as she carefully lifts a French fry from the dish.

After lunch, Tsz Yan and her father head for the markets while her mother goes upstairs to the grocery store. Father and daughter buy fruits and treats, all from Lai Man's list. Then they buy flowers for Lai Man, which were not on the list. Tsz Yan wonders if the flower lady has any edelweiss to sell. She and her father walk through the markets, looking at shirts, shoes, food, plumbing equipment, all sorts of things. They stop on the way out to look at the live chickens and ducks waiting to be picked for dinner. Ever since she was small, Tsz Yan has always stopped to see the doomed chickens.

Sunday means dim sum, and it also means family visits. On Sunday, the Laws always try to see some of their big family. This day they take a bus to Kwai Chung to see Tsz Yan's father's family. The bus carries them along a road between the hills of Hong Kong and the always-there, always-busy sea. It is the same road Tsz Yan's mother travels to work every day. Tsz Yan tries not to think about the road that will carry her father back to China in the morning.

Her family is the last to arrive, joining her father's big family in his youngest sister's not-so-big apartment. Tsz Yan greets her grand-

mother, who smiles at the family all around. Aunts and uncles sit around the living room table, which is piled high with food. There are spring rolls, sushi, chicken wings, chicken feet, fruit salad, jellyfish, and lots more. One of the smaller cousins keeps feeding jellyfish to the dog, but only when the aunts are not looking.

Tsz Yan stops for a moment to join three cousins watching a Jackie Chan movie on the giant television. Jackie Chan is a movie star and a hero to most boys in Hong Kong, to some girls, and to a lot of adults. Tsz Yan thinks about this as she watches her uncle

pretending to listen to the other adults while he is really watching Jackie Chan be brave and funny.

Tsz Yan leaves her cousins to the movie. She and her older cousin, Kwan Poi, climb on a bed to play a card game with the English name Uno. They are always interrupted by the youngest cousins, who are playing a video game on a tiny television and need a bigger cousin to restart it. The card game is almost ruined by other cousins who jump into the room pretending they are Jackie Chan fighting bad guys. Two aunts have to crowd into the small room as the good guys begin to battle each other.

Later, the grown-ups drink cups of warm ginseng tea. It smells terrible to Tsz Yan—not like the smell of the warm-from-the-oven, sweet yellow raisin cake, which calls everyone to one room for eating, watching television, singing, and telling family stories again.

The afternoon begins to wind down. Aunts, uncles, and cousins

head home. Since they are more than halfway there, Tsz Yan's parents decide to go by bus to Kowloon for a short visit with Tsz Yan's mother's parents. During the ride, Tsz Yan quietly practices "Old MacDonald Had a Farm," a singing-team song. She wonders why, with twenty-six letters to choose from, the song only uses E-I-E-I-O. And she wonders if this man MacDonald is related to the hamburger man McDonald. Their names sound the same.

Heading from the bus to her grandparents' apartment, Tsz Yan's family walks through the bustling streets of Kowloon. The signs for the shops are so many and so crowded that they connect one side

of the street to the other overhead. Tsz Yan thinks they look like bridges for birds. Her grandparents live on the second floor.

Tsz Yan's family greets more of her family. Her grandmother, grandfather, uncle, and new aunt live in the apartment together. Her father joins her uncle and grandfather in watching a soccer game. Her mother and aunt exchange news. Tsz Yan happily follows her grandmother, who always has something for Tsz Yan to do. In the kitchen, Tsz Yan helps her grandmother fix dinner. She stirs her grandmother's special soup, made with vegetables and Chinese

herbs. Her grandmother knows the soup will help keep Tsz Yan and the rest of the family healthy. Then Tsz Yan counts her grandfather's cacti, the ones he grows with great care in the apartment window.

The game over, the soup eaten, the talk ended, Yi Fau is anxious to head home to Tuen Mun. Tsz Yan wonders why her father is in such a hurry to have her do her homework. She is not in such a big rush.

Back home, under Minnie's watchful eye, Tsz Yan sits at her table to finish. Only two more words. . . . She writes NOISY once, and again. Tsz Yan thinks NOISY is easy. NOISY is three boys watching a Jackie Chan movie, each one adding his own fighting sounds to the already loud movie. NOISY is the sound of everyone clapping and cheering as the killer whale and his friend leap high into the sky at Ocean Park. And the biggest NOISY of all is the happy noise as everyone eats, talks, laughs, and calls out for more dim sum on a Sunday morning. NOISY.

And, finally, the last word: FAMILY. A good Sunday word, Tsz Yan realizes. FAMILY is her father's seven brothers and sisters and their children. And her mother's brothers and sister, and Tsz Yan's best friend, her cousin Ho Ying, who is both FAMILY and FRIEND. FAMILY is her pretty new aunt and her wise grandmother and grandfather living in busy Kowloon. And FAMILY is her

mother, father, and Tsz Yan, all together for the weekend. Finally, Tsz Yan finishes her English homework.

Now there's only a little time left of her weekend. A little time before Yi Fau leaves again, before Lai Man and Tsz Yan begin their week of work and school and homework once again. Looking at her work with her father, Tsz Yan remembers the math homework. All in a worry, she calls a classmate to talk about the assignment.

Tsz Yan tries to pay attention to her math, counting squares and numbers the way she should. But the English homework fills up her mind. She remembers the HUNGRY turtle FAMILY swimming over to see their new FRIEND who was maybe a little SCARED to feed them. Tsz Yan remembers the NOISY girls who were feeding the HUNGRY pigeons and remembers too that she was a little worried they might laugh at her for being afraid—like the boy in the story!

Tsz Yan counts squares over and down and fills them in. But then she finds herself wondering about the little boy who was so SCARED of his bicycle, wondering if he is outside right now, pedaling around. She thinks she hears a NOISY soccer game; maybe her FRIEND Ka Kit is playing. Wishing she could be outside playing, Tsz Yan knows that her FAMILY will not be HAPPY if she does not finish her homework. She tries hard to think math thoughts. Slow and steady, she gets the work done, but all the while her new words sing, sing, sing through her mind.

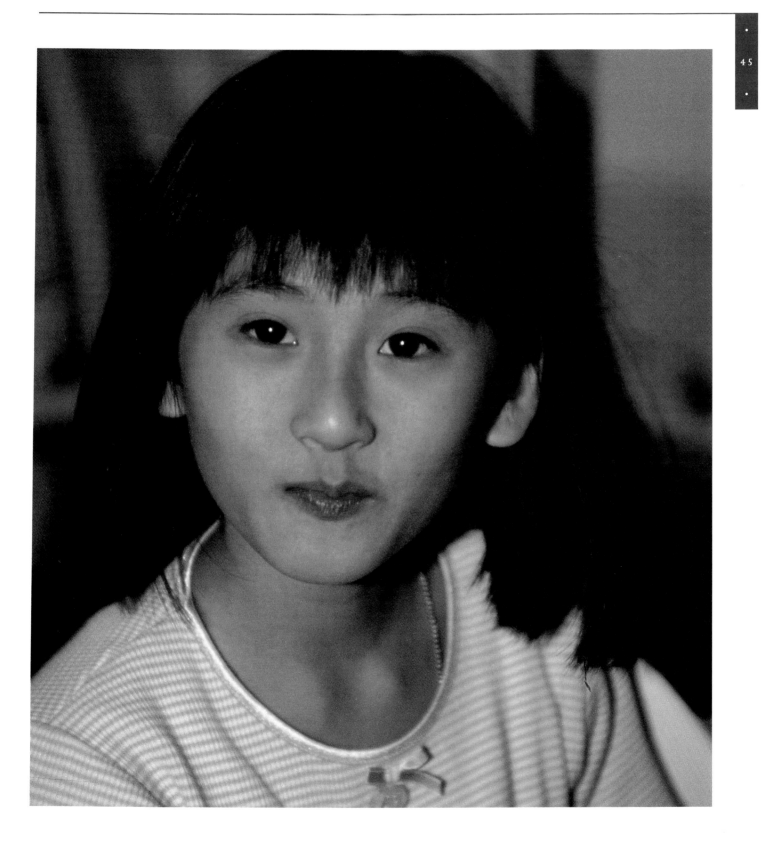